Mark Haddon

Polar Bears

Methuen Drama

Published by Methuen Drama 2010

1 3 5 7 9 10 8 6 4 2

Methuen Drama
A & C Black Publishers Limited
36 Soho Square
London W1D 3QY
www.methuendrama.com

ISBN: 978 1 408 13084 1

A CIP catalogue record for this book
is available from the British Library

Typeset by Country Setting, Kingsdown, Kent
Printed and bound in Great Britain by
CPI Cox & Wyman Ltd, Reading, Berkshire

Polar Bears

Polar Bears was first performed at the Donmar Warehouse, London, on 1 April 2010. The cast, in order of appearance, was as follows:

Sandy	Paul Hilton
John	Richard Coyle
Kay	Jodhi May
Margaret	Celia Imrie
Jesus	David Leon
Girl	Skye Bennett / Alice Sykes

Director Jamie Lloyd
Designer Soutra Gilmour
Lighting Designer Jon Clark
Composers and Sound Designers Ben and Max Ringham

The playscript that follows was correct at time of going to press, but might have changed during rehearsal.

Characters

Sandy
John
Kay
Margaret
Jesus
Girl

One

Sandy *and* **John** *enter.*

Sandy Sorry. I'm going on about myself.

John No. It's good to listen to a human voice. It's been a while. Helps calm me down.

Sandy John?

John Thanks. Thanks for coming.

Sandy John, what's the matter?

John I don't really know where to start.

Sandy Is this the disciplinary stuff at college?

John What? Oh, no, it's nothing to do with that.

Sandy So, what is it then?

John I'm so sorry about this.

Sandy Just tell me, OK.

John I shouldn't have called you.

Sandy I'm family. You're meant to call me.

John I suspect you're not going to think of me as family after this. In fact, technically, I'm not sure I count as family any longer.

Sandy Are you having an affair?

John No. I'm not having an affair. I've never had an affair. Never thought about having an affair. Which is pretty amazing, don't you think? In the circumstances.

Sandy Is Kay having an affair?

John No, Kay's not having an affair. Or rather, she wasn't. I'm pretty sure she wasn't. It's hard to be certain about that kind of thing.

Sandy Has something happened in Oslo?

John   Kay's not in Oslo.

Sandy   No?

John   Have you got a cigarette?

Sandy   Sure.

He gives **John** *a cigarette.*

John   Thanks.

Sandy   So where is she?

John   She's in the cellar.

Sandy   What's she doing in the cellar?

John   She's dead.

Sandy   You said she was in the cellar.

John   She's dead. And she's in the cellar.

Sandy   What are you talking about?

John   Ironically, she didn't kill herself. If that's what you're thinking.

Sandy   Whoa, John. Don't fuck around like this.

John   You see, actually, I killed her.

Pause.

Sandy   You're serious.

John   We had a fight. Like we do, periodically. I pushed her and she fell. There was such a small amount of blood. You expect there to be a lot of blood, don't you? From seeing people being killed on the television.

Sandy   Oh, Christ.

He starts to exit.

John   Please, Sandy. Don't.

Pause.

She's a bit of a mess. You go stiff after a bit and I had to kind of fold her to get her down the stairs. I think I might have broken something. She doesn't smell too good, either.

Pause.

Sandy   What the fuck have you done?

John   I'm really sorry.

Sandy   You killed my sister.

John   I keep thinking that if I concentrate hard enough I can make time go backwards. Like Superman flying round the earth really fast so the San Andreas Fault opens up again and he can pull Lois Lane's car out of the ground. Except I'm not Superman. And I can't make time go backwards.

Sandy   Shut up.

He takes his mobile out.

John   Don't, Sandy. Please.

Sandy *can't get through.*

Sandy   Fuck.

John   Sorry. The reception's rubbish.

Sandy   Why didn't you call an ambulance?

Pause.

Answer the fucking question.

John   I'm sorry. I thought . . . Well . . . She was dead.

Sandy   Why didn't you call an ambulance?

John   I did a first-aid course at college. Only a couple of months ago, funnily enough. I gave her chest massage. And mouth-to-mouth resuscitation.

Sandy   I asked you why you didn't –

John   Her heart had stopped. Three minutes without oxygen and the brain starts to die. We're a long way from the nearest hospital, Sandy.

Sandy   What if there was an ambulance nearby? She was lying on the floor, dying. What if one was just passing? If there was a million to one chance . . .

John   To tell the truth I didn't want someone to come and take her away.

Sandy   So you put her in the cellar?

John   You see, then I would have been on my own. And I didn't want to be on my own.

Sandy   This can't be true.

John   Those were exactly the words I kept saying to myself.

Sandy   I'm going to ring the police.

John   This was a few days ago, incidentally. Which accounts for my dishevelled state. And the smell down there.

Sandy   How many days ago?

John   Four, maybe five. I've lost track of time, rather. I rang Sian at the faculty office and told them there was a family crisis. I guess this counts as a family crisis. That's why I put her in the bag. It's what the hall carpet was delivered in. I was going to throw it away but Kay said we should hang on to it in case it ever came in handy. You know what Kay was like about recycling. Please. Don't ring the police.

Sandy   You're asking me to pretend this didn't happen?

John   We can sort it out. If we just stay calm and think it through really carefully.

Sandy   We can't 'sort it out'. This is not something you 'sort out'.

John   Also . . . it wasn't really an accident.

Sandy   No, John. No.

John   I just got very angry. You know what Kay's like.

Sandy   What did you do?

John I wanted to hurt her. And just for a second . . . I wanted it to be over. Don't we all imagine that kind of thing sometimes?

Sandy No, we don't all imagine that kind of thing sometimes.

John You don't live with Kay.

Sandy I'm ringing the police.

He exits.

John Maybe she said she was going to Oslo but she didn't go. I mean, obviously, she didn't go. But maybe she went somewhere else. Maybe she committed suicide. I mean, that's not exactly out of the question, is it?

Sandy *enters.*

Sandy Where's the phone?

John I was thinking. Maybe you could help me bury her. On Oakshott Hill.

Sandy Tell me where the fucking phone is or I swear I'll –

John Fallen trunks and mushrooms and this dappled light. And bluebells. Like this great wave of blue just swept in.

Sandy Where's the phone?

John It's in the kitchen.

Sandy *exits.*

John Kay always said she wanted to be buried there. I mean, not in the immediate future. I think she was planning something a little further off. Except, of course, you can't be buried there. Because it's a country park. You can have your ashes scattered there. You can have your ashes scattered anywhere. I think. But you could be buried there unofficially.

Sandy *enters.*

John Because she does wander, Sandy. You know that.

Sandy   You cut the cord.

John   With the kitchen scissors.

Pause.

It was a lot tougher than I expected.

Sandy   John . . . ?

Pause.

John   I really need you to help me, Sandy.

Sandy   I'm leaving.

John   You can't leave, Sandy.

Sandy   And how are you going to stop me?

Two

Kay I saw *The Scream* yesterday. The famous one by Munch.
The man standing on the bridge doing that Janet Leigh pose
from *Psycho*. These two dark figures in the background. 'My
friends walked on and I was left in fear with an open wound
in my chest.' Unquote. This swirly, blood-red sky. You can feel
the horror. Plus he's looking at you. It's like you're frightening
him. Or whatever's standing behind you.

So I skipped the Viking Ship Museum because I was obviously
going to be freaked out by the idea of being raped and having
my house burnt down and I took a boat trip out into the
Oslofjord, which is the fjord in the background of *The Scream*.
All these islands with little wooden summer houses. Very
Ingmar Bergman. And the ruins of this Early Christian
monastery. Except the monks had to get up at dawn and go
to bed at dusk, which was kind of inconvenient because it's a
three-hour night in the summer and a three-hour day in the
winter. And it took six years to get a rule change from the
Pope. On account of not having Ryanair.

I'm sorry. Things just build up. I need this cold wind to blow
stuff away. I lie awake in the night. Dirty-orange light through
the curtains. Pipes clicking in the wall. I get so scared. And
there's a pull to the north, isn't there? Zigzag jumpers and
reindeer. Everything simpler and cleaner.

I'm thinking of flying to Svalbard. Over the hills and far
away. Longyearbyen Glacier. The turquoise waters of
Magdalenefjord. Whales, seals, walruses. Actual polar bears.
There's this vault. They dug this tunnel into a mountain. Ten
thousand seed samples, all kept below freezing. So if everything
else is wiped out there's this cradle far away. So nothing will
be lost. I find it hard to talk about without crying . . . You
have to take tours with a guide. Because of the polar bears.
You need a gun, tripwires, flares. All that kind of stuff. But
I'm not sure I could stand the company. Because people talk
when it's night-time and there's nothing for hundreds of
miles. Gather round the fire and share stories. I couldn't take

that. Not right now. So I might just get a tent and crampons and go on my own. But it's all right because no one's been killed by a polar bear since 1995. Real darkness, though. Imagine that. The sky so clear there's hardly any black between the stars. Just this fine white powder . . . You understand, don't you? I love you. I really do. I just find it hard to hang on to that sometimes. I find it hard to hang on to me. I need to strip everything back. Dig into the mountain and find the seeds.

I'll call again later. I really do think I'll call again later.

Three

Living room. **Margaret** *and* **John**.

Margaret   There's a little river beyond the houses. The garden used to go all the way down to the bank. This endless slope of green. Sandy and his friends would build ramps at the bottom and cycle as fast as they could and try to reach the other side. One boy lost four teeth. I forget his name. There were two stands of poplars, one to either side. You could see the woods. Kay used to like me telling stories of the creatures that lived there. Foxes, badgers, bears. It's all gone now. The view. The river. The poplars. I had to sell the land a few years ago . . .

Pause.

She told you about her father . . . ?

John   Yes. Yes she did.

Margaret   Out there in the hallway. Hanging from the banisters. Everyone told me I should move. But you can't run away. You have to face it. Might as well face it in a place you know. His father ended his life in an asylum. It's like those Greek tragedies where a curse gets handed down from generation to generation.

John   The *Oresteia* . . .

Pause.

Aeschylus.

Pause.

Agamemnon sacrifices his daughter Iphigenia in return for a fair wind to Troy. His wife Clytemnestra kills him when he returns home. Then her son, Orestes, kills her to avenge his father's death and is pursued by the Furies . . .

Margaret   I used to be a teacher, Mr Carr.

John   Yes. I'm sorry . . . But the curse was lifted in the end, wasn't it? After the intercession of Athena.

Margaret   You read these old plays and you think it's just something people did two, three thousand years ago. Gods and monsters. Historical interest. And then you realise, nothing changes.

John   Well, some things change. I mean, the maenads, for example.

Margaret   The what?

John   Bands of women inspired by Dionysus into a wild orgiastic frenzy of drinking and lewd sexual behaviour in which they tore wild animals apart and ate their flesh raw.

Margaret   You've led a very quiet life, haven't you?

Kay enters.

Kay   Is she giving you the curse thing?

John   Well . . .

Kay   Some mothers do the weather and 'How was your journey?' Mine does how her daughter's going to end up in Broadmoor because Daddy was bonkers and Grandpa ran naked down Kidlington High Street.

John   Unless the Goddess of Wisdom intercedes at the last minute.

Margaret   Kay is ill, John. You may think she's high-spirited. But it's a disease.

John   Margaret . . .

Margaret   What?

John   Kay is standing right here.

Margaret   So I should talk about these things behind her back?

John   I didn't mean that.

Margaret   Kay knows what I think. She also knows I'm right.

Kay   This woman could be your mother-in-law.

Margaret   This month is a good month. But there are bad months. Sometimes Kay has to go into hospital.

John   I know.

Kay   We've been seeing one another for three months. Amazingly it has come up in conversation.

Margaret   Talking means nothing. Not until you've seen it. Not until you've been there.

Kay   She's a great saleswoman, isn't she?

John   Margaret, listen . . . Mrs Lewis. You're right. I have led a very quiet life. I'm not an exciting person. I don't have moods in the way that Kay has moods.

Margaret   Moods?

Kay   Shut up and listen to him.

John   I suspect you think I'm rather boring. I suspect most people think I'm boring. But it's Kay's opinion that matters. And when I'm with Kay I'm special. I have this quality she doesn't have. I'm stable. Around most people it's invisible, but with Kay . . . I'm the person holding the bottom of the kite string. I do something she can't do. And I think we all want to be special.

Kay *kisses him.*

Kay   I love you so much.

Doorbell.

Margaret   That will be Sandy.

Kay   Oh joy.

Margaret *exits.*

Kay   I told you. She's never going to like you.

John   I didn't know she used to be a teacher.

Kay   Sandy's not going to like you either. I'd brace yourself for being patronised and insulted.

John   Why did you invite him?

Kay   Mum did. Possibly so he'll patronise and insult you and you'll head for the hills.

John   Well, I'm really looking forward to this.

Kay   On the positive side, he's not very intelligent.

John   Except that it's not actually a quiz.

Kay   We don't have to see either of them again, if you don't want to. I mean, I probably do, but you don't.

Sandy *enters.*

John   The infamous Sandy.

Sandy   John.

They shake hands.

Kay   I'd better help Mum in the kitchen.

John   Are you going?

Kay   Good luck.

She exits.

Pause.

John   Kay says Margaret invited you so you'd patronise and insult me and I'd head for the hills.

Pause.

You make supermarket checkouts.

Sandy   Not personally.

John   No, but . . .

Sandy   Actually, we don't do the big-scale hardware any more. We sold that side of the business six months ago. We've moved into hand-held point-of-sale systems. Restaurants,

mainly. The wireless unit the waitress brings to your table.
Sends your order to the kitchen. Keeps your tab. Every table
visible on every unit. Lets you pay at the table without your
card being taken out back to be copied by some dodgy
Albanian. We're working on programs to detect and disable
zappers at the moment.

John   Zappers?

Sandy   Automated sales suppression devices. Computer
programs that skim off a proportion of the sales and keep
them off the books so you pay less sales tax. Germany's about
to mandate tamper-proof POS systems, so it's only a matter
of time before the law's changed over here. Obviously no
one's going to want these systems till then. I mean, who's
going to buy a car that forces you to drive below the speed
limit? But when it changes, bam! We want to be first out of
the gate.

John   Sounds interesting.

Sandy   No, it's not, John. It's bloody boring.

John   Well, you know, you've been pretty successful at it, so
I guess you must find it interesting.

Sandy   People become millionaires selling gravel.

John   Point taken.

Sandy   What interests me is taking risks, doing deals, happy
shareholders, consistent revenue and income growth, a
beautiful wife, two boys in a private school and a Jaguar XK
which is almost but not quite as beautiful as Laura. Apparently
you teach philosophy.

John   Which interests me. Quite a lot.

Sandy   And is no use to anyone whatsoever.

John   I'm not going to rise to the bait.

Sandy   Go on. Rise to the bait. It's much more fun.

John   Let's not do this.

Sandy   Come on. You're a philosopher. You like arguments. Show me your stuff.

John   Philosophy is more than liking an argument. That's just being down the pub.

Sandy   You see? We're up and running.

John   Plus, I don't think you really want an argument.

Sandy   Well, I'm enjoying it so far.

John   At least not one about philosophy.

Sandy   Try me.

Pause.

John   Well, I could start by giving you a list of all the philosophers who've shaped the way we see the world. Aristotle, who invented formal logic. Democritus, who said the world was composed of atoms. Descartes, who laid the foundations for the natural sciences so that we can put men on the moon and remove brain tumours and use hand-held point-of-sale systems in Beefeater steakhouses.

Sandy   Touché, baby.

John   But you'd be ready with some snappy rejoinder like 'Touché, baby' because you're not really interested.

Sandy   This is more like it.

John   Philosophy isn't about being clever or better informed. It's not about being right. It's about the possibility that you might be wrong. It's about asking questions, all the time. How do you solve this problem? Is it the right problem? What am I trying to achieve?

Sandy   So what are we trying to achieve here?

John   You're trying to make me feel uncomfortable and I'm trying to prevent you from succeeding too much.

Pause.

Sandy   You won't last long.

John Ad hominem.

Sandy That's a big word.

John Actually, it's two. 'Against the man.' It means you're changing the subject by attacking the person who disagrees with you.

Sandy There was this one guy. God knows where she picked him up. Rock festival. Sainsbury's. Soup kitchen. Long hair, beard. Now, there's one thing you have to understand about my sister. I can be a selfish bastard sometimes. I have to be a selfish bastard sometimes. But she's the queen. When the moon's in the right phase. So this guy moves in. Mum comes back from a weekend with her sister and this prick is making breakfast in the kitchen in his underwear. Mum has absolutely no idea who he is. He's here for a week and they're fucking like monkeys upstairs. And this guy *smelt*. I know because Mum rang me and I had to drop everything and hightail it up here and kick him and all his crap out the front door.

Pause.

Come on. We were having fun.

John No. You're having fun. Actually, I'm not sure you are having fun. To be honest, I'm not sure what you're feeling. I don't meet many people like you.

Sandy He didn't even turn round. He just picked up his things and buggered off with his tails between his legs. They all do eventually. You won't be any different.

John Why do you dislike me so much? You only met me a few minutes ago.

Sandy Because you're weak. Because you're exactly the kind of man Kay goes for. Someone she can wrap around her little finger. You think you can sort everything out by being nice. Except you can't. And when you find out you can't, you fuck off and leave someone else to pick up the pieces.

John I'm not weak.

Sandy   Of course you're weak. If you weren't you'd have punched my lights out by now.

Kay *enters.*

Kay   So, how are you two getting on?

John *punches* **Sandy**.

Kay   Holy shit.

John   I'm not weak. I was just working out how to solve the problem.

Kay (*to* **John**)   Are you OK?

John   I feel rather good, actually. (*To* **Sandy**.) Are you planning to hit me back?

Margaret *enters.*

Margaret   What on earth is happening in here?

Pause.

Sandy   He's all right, this one.

Four

Kay at a café table in a train station. Jesus enters with two coffees and a flapjack.

Jesus   They didn't have any apple things so I got you a flapjack. One sugar, no milk, is that right?

Kay   This is really good of you.

Jesus   It's no problem. Cigarette?

Kay   No thanks. I don't smoke. I mean, I smoke sometimes. OK, I'll have a cigarette.

They smoke.

I was expecting you to be a lot more Jewish.

Jesus   'Wide is the gate and broad is the way that leadeth to destruction and many there be that go in thereat . . . ' It's not Philip Roth, is it? This was two thousand years ago. Jewish was different back then. Everything was different back then. If I remember correctly you were having your arses kicked by the Romans. And not a Yorkshire pudding or a pint of warm beer in sight . . . How are you doing, kid?

Kay   This is good.

Jesus   I meant, how are *you* doing? Not, 'What does the food taste like?'

Kay   Better. I think. It's hard to tell.

Pause.

So you spent forty days in the wilderness.

Jesus   Bitter herbs and rainwater. Seriously, I do not recommend it.

Kay   And Satan appeared to you.

Jesus   After forty days of bitter herbs and rainwater pretty much everything starts appearing to you. The polar bears. They were the ones that really freaked me out.

Kay   Did they hurt you?

Jesus It was the desert, Kay. There were no polar bears.

Kay Oh, yeah. But you had to undergo temptation.

Jesus This guy appears out of nowhere. Black wings. Sneery little voice. Turn this stone into bread. Throw yourself off that mountain and let the angels catch you.

Kay So you'd commit two of the seven deadly sins.

Jesus The whole point of going into the desert is not eating bread. If I wanted bread I'd go to a shop. As for throwing yourself off a mountain and letting the angels catch you . . . Does that sound tempting? Or am I missing something?

Kay Throwing yourself off a mountain and actually hitting the ground. That sounds tempting. You know, at certain phases of the moon.

Jesus Anyway, the seven deadly sins aren't even mentioned in the Bible.

Kay No?

Jesus Fourth-century monk. Evagrius Ponticus. Now there was a miserable bastard. You found a new religion. Open-door policy. Prostitutes. Sinners. Non-Jews. All we ask is purity of heart. I thought it was a rather good idea myself. But it all goes the same way in the end. I'm pure of heart. You're not. So I'm going to burn you at the stake.

Kay Do you ever get depressed?

Jesus The cross thing was not good.

Kay You look pretty relaxed in the pictures.

Jesus I was turning the other cheek.

Kay But it still hurt?

Jesus They drove nails through my feet, Kay.

Kay Well, I'm impressed. If that was me I'd be screaming the house down.

Pause.

There's this fear. It comes out of nowhere. And I know it's just chemicals. I know the whole thing is chemicals. Love. Grief. That ache in your chest when you see a baby. But it feels so real, doesn't it? And when you're in the grip of the black stuff, that feels real, too. Because you're inside this head. There's nowhere else to be . . . Sometimes I imagine everything falling apart. Global warming. Nuclear war. Really big meteorite, dust clouds blocking out the sun for years. All the plants and trees and animals dying off. Stuck in a basement eating tinned food. Scurvy. Lice. Cholera. Guns and tyre-fires and looting. Gangs of young men roaming the streets looking for supplies. Killing the weaker men and raping the women because, you know, why not? Who's going to stop you? Eating kids when the dogs have run out. Their little burnt faces turning on a spit.

Jesus I bet you're fun at a party.

Kay I'm actually really good at a party . . . Why did the pervert cross the road?

Jesus I don't know. Why did the pervert cross the road?

Kay Because he was stuck in the chicken.

No reaction.

I guess you have to know the original chicken joke.

Pause.

You meet someone new. You tell them a funny story. You tell them a sad story. It's like the two of you are playing music. And if you get the tuning and the timing just right it soars.

Jesus Tell me a sad story.

Kay I thought I could get away. From me. From John. From my mother. From the gas bill and the dirty laundry. From all those sad faces you see in shopping centres. And then you do get away and you realise that you're still you.

Jesus The gas bill and the dirty laundry. They're important. They're what we're here for.

Kay   I thought we were here for, you know, honouring your father and mother and not killing people and stopping to look after the injured man on the other side of the road.

Jesus   Yeah, we're here for that, too.

Kay   But, you know, shouldn't we be making it a better world?

Jesus   Every month forty-five thousand people die in the Congo. Disease. Starvation. Civil war. People are selfish and angry and stupid and often completely incapable of understanding the suffering of others. It really will end in the basement with the tinned food and the gangs. Not for you, maybe. But for your grandchildren. Or your grandchildren's grandchildren. I mean, where else is it going to end? And there won't be anyone handing out certificates for good behaviour.

Kay   You're not so much fun now.

Jesus   We all get nails driven through our feet. *Eloi, Eloi, lama sabachthani?* 'My God, my God, why have you forsaken me?' You can scream the house down or you can look good in the pictures. Anyway, fun isn't really my thing . . . You'll miss your train.

Kay   I thought you were going to help me.

Jesus   There are people who love you. They're the people who have to help you.

Kay   Will I see you again?

Jesus   Other people need me.

Kay   I thought you might be like Santa Claus. You know, two billion chimneys in one night.

Pause.

Sorry. Maybe that was a bit . . .

Jesus   You've got to go.

Five

Kay *shows her artwork to* **John**. *We can't see it.*

Kay This is the part where the girl and the monster are flying over the hills at night.

John It's wonderful. I mean, really. The sky. How do you do that?

Kay I keep a camera in my bag. I take photographs of thrown-away dolls, stains on walls, stuff in skips. I print the photos on paper. Paint them. Burn them. Leave them in the rain . . . This is the wallpaper in a house they were knocking down round the corner.

John Your mum talked about it like it was a hobby.

Kay She was an artist.

John I thought she was a teacher.

Kay She taught art.

John And she doesn't want you to be an artist.

Kay She did watercolours and woodcuts. I used to think she was a genius when I was little because she never went over the lines. She could draw a circle without using a compass. She looks at this and she doesn't get it . . . Art's all about going over the lines.

John But she doesn't paint now.

Kay She's terrified of finding she can't do it any more. And she can see time getting shorter.

John Well, you can certainly do it.

Kay Sometimes. I'd almost finished the book at the end of last year. I was thinking, this is the one. Publishers are going to love this. How could they not? It's brilliant.

John It is.

Kay   Then the darkness came down and I realised I was an idiot. Why would anyone in their right mind pay money for this? It's messy, it doesn't hang together, and this story, it'd scare the living daylights out of most children.

John   Kids love being scared.

Kay   I was ashamed of it, and I was even more ashamed of being a fool for thinking it was any good.

John   That's ridiculous.

Kay   Then I met you and the darkness lifted. Or maybe the darkness lifted which meant I actually talked to you when we met and you didn't run away in horror, and a few weeks later I took these out of the drawer and I realised they were good.

John   Are you sending them off to publishers?

Kay   Walker want to bring it out in September.

John   Bloody hell. You kept that quiet. You should be jumping up and down.

Kay   I keep thinking if I tell everyone I'll get a second letter saying it was a clerical error.

John   Do you want me to read the first? You know, to reassure you that it's not scrawled in green ink and capital letters.

Kay   No, it's OK. I realise I'm being silly. I'm just not used to good things happening. It's going to take a little while getting used to it.

John   I'm jealous.

Kay   Don't be daft.

John   I've written twelve journal articles that will be read by thirty-one people then sit in the stacks of the Bodleian Library till Doomsday. And a slim book on epistemology that requires a mortgage to buy it.

Kay   But you teach people.

John   And if I'm really lucky one day there'll be a chief constable or an antiques dealer and they'll say to someone at a cocktail party, I had this great tutor who showed me the importance of thinking clearly. Whereas you . . . in twenty, fifty, a hundred years' time, someone is going to take this off a shelf and sit their son or daughter on their lap . . .

Kay   Will you keep on loving me? When it goes dark again?

Six

Kay *in a foetal position.* **John** *nearby with a mug of tea.*

John Hey you.

He touches her.

Kay (*shouts*) Don't touch me. Just . . . don't touch me.

John OK . . . I'll stay over here.

Pause.

I'm not going to hurt you, Kay. I would never hurt you. You understand that, don't you?

Kay Shit, shit, shit.

John Can I get you anything? A cup of tea, maybe.

Pause.

Have you taken any Valium?

Kay Stop fucking patronising me. Stop treating me like a fucking child.

John Look. I've made you a cup of tea. I'll just leave it next to you and fetch a couple of Valium.

Kay *smashes the mug.*

Kay Go. Away.

Pause.

Sandy *appears. He is invisible to* **Kay**.

Sandy I was the one who found him.

John Found who?

Sandy My father. In the hallway.

John Kay said she found him.

Sandy Yeah, well. Some people like to be the centre of attention, don't they? I was eight years old. And the thing

I noticed first was that he'd wet himself. And his bowels had
opened. Which is, apparently, not uncommon. It was dripping
out of the bottom of his trousers. On to the phone table. I
can still see it. And I was disgusted. I knew that he was dead.
I could see the rope and the way his neck was bent. And the
way his face bloated and was covered in this huge bruise.
But it was the disgust. That was the big thing. And the
embarrassment. That my father had gone to the toilet in the
hallway.

John   You were eight years old.

Sandy   And that haunted me. Not my father dying. But
feeling the wrong thing. Feeling something shallow and trivial
about me, instead of something deep and honourable about
him.

John   You were a child.

Sandy   She thinks she's the only one. But even now
sometimes I wake up in the middle of the night . . .

John   Everyone has nightmares, Sandy. This is not a
nightmare. This is Kay's life.

Sandy   This is play-acting, John.

John   Don't you dare –

Sandy   It's like alcoholism. The romance of fucking
everything up. Life is bloody hard work sometimes. I've been
there. You can keep going. Or you can reach for that bottle.
You can let the voices win. You can say, I don't want to be
here any more.

John   It's a disease.

Sandy   And as soon as you say that magic word, hey presto!
You're the victim. Have some pills. See this nice doctor. You
don't have to do a proper job. You don't have to look after
yourself. Other people will look after you.

John   Have you ever been in a psychiatric hospital?

Sandy   Three meals a day and a bed for the night and people asking, 'How are you feeling today?' Come on. If she was really unlucky she'd be homeless. Living under a bridge with hepatitis and bunch of smack addicts for mates. If she was really unlucky she'd be in a wheelchair. Trust me, John, a psychiatric hospital is like a fucking hotel.

John   You have no idea.

Sandy   You're just the next lifeline. You're the reason she can still pull this stuff. You and my mother. And you love it because it makes you feel so important.

John   You only ever think about yourself, don't you?

Sandy   She's a child. She's a child because no one's told her it's time to grow up.

Pause.

John   Why is she so frightened of me, Sandy?

Sandy   I have no bloody idea.

John   What happened to her?

Sandy   Nothing happened to her.

John   Because when this happens to her, the one thing that terrifies her is that I'm going to hurt her. And I would never hurt her. And when she thinks I might hurt her, it makes me feel sick. Where's does that come from? Why is she frightened, Sandy?

Sandy   You want me to say I beat her up as a kid? You want me to say her father abused her? That would be so easy, wouldn't it? One more thing that's someone else's fault. One more thing that's been visited on her.

John   You haven't answered my question.

Sandy   Maybe she knows it makes you feel sick. Maybe that's the string she can pull. She's not stupid.

John   She's your sister. She tried to kill herself.

Sandy   If she'd wanted to kill herself she might have tried a bit harder. It's a cry for attention.

John   And if you're walking beside a river and you see someone drowning and they're calling out for help, what do you say, Sandy? It's just a cry for attention? Some people need attention. Some people really are drowning.

Kay *begins to cry.*

John *goes over and holds her.*

Kay   I'm sorry. I'm so sorry.

Sandy   You bloody idiot.

Seven

Kitchen. **Margaret** *and* **Sandy**.

Sandy You have to leave.

Margaret You've been saying that for years.

Sandy I can't afford it any more.

Margaret Don't be ridiculous.

Sandy Things have changed.

Margaret You're bullying me.

Sandy You've got buckets in the drawing room. It's like the bloody Amazon rainforest in there.

Margaret Mr Bannister's recovering from an operation.

Sandy He's eighty, for fuck's sake.

Margaret He's seventy-one and there's no need to use that kind of language.

Sandy Here's a radical idea. You get an actual builder.

Margaret We've known Mr Bannister for a long time.

Sandy You've known your postman for a long time but you wouldn't get him to fix your roof. I am not paying to keep you in a half-derelict five-bedroomed house in the middle of bloody nowhere.

Margaret I don't need your money.

Sandy You'll end up as one of those crazy old women who sleeps by the fire because upstairs is knee-deep in cat shit.

Margaret This is my home.

Sandy It's twelve miles into town. There's no post office. There's one bus.

Margaret I can drive.

Sandy You hit a wall.

Margaret   That was not my fault.

Sandy   When did you last speak to someone?

Margaret   Kay rang yesterday.

Sandy   In person.

Pause.

You could die here and no one would find you for a week.

Margaret   What do you mean, 'Things have changed'?

Sandy   Laura wants a divorce. And don't you dare say you're sorry because it's exactly what you predicted.

Margaret   Are you OK?

Sandy   What do you think?

Margaret   I honestly don't know, Sandy.

Sandy   We were talking about the house.

Margaret   Will I get to see the boys?

Sandy   I'll have them every other weekend, and as Laura points out, I'm bollocks at parenting, so I suspect I'll be bringing them to see you quite a bit.

Pause.

Margaret   I feel so old . . . There's this moment when the whole world starts to feel like a foreign country, and you realise you're never going home.

Sandy   Stop being so bloody dramatic. Your daughter's found a bloke and I'm offering to buy you a flat. It's not cancer.

Margaret   I'm so lonely.

Sandy   Kids leave home. Or we'd have died out several million years ago.

Margaret   At night especially.

Sandy   You've spent the last fifteen years wishing she'd look after herself and now you want her back?

Margaret   She's my daughter.

Sandy   Daughters grow up and become someone else's problem.

Margaret   I always liked Laura.

Sandy   No you didn't. You felt sorry for her because she was married to me. You thought she was a trophy wife. She *was* a trophy wife. Scales from my eyes. Waking up and smelling the coffee. All that shit. Still, you learn, don't you? Won't be making that mistake again.

Margaret   I doubt anyone will give you the chance to make that mistake again.

Sandy   Thanks for the vote of confidence.

Margaret   I worry about you, too, you know.

Sandy   No you don't. You worry about the fact that you don't have to worry about me. You worry about the fact that I don't need you.

Margaret   I worry about the fact that you don't really care about other people.

Sandy   I employ sixty-five people. I make that company work so they get paid and they go home and feed their kids and buy a house and run a car and go on holiday. You can call it what you like, but caring counts for bugger all if you haven't got a job.

Margaret   You're still my little boy.

Sandy   You have to leave.

Eight

Kay Once upon a time there was a beautiful woman who lived in a house by a river. She was married to a brave soldier who died protecting his comrades in a distant country. On the day the beautiful woman heard the news she also discovered she was pregnant. So half of her was happy and half of her was sad.

The beautiful woman gave birth to twins and because she was half sad and half happy one of the twins was a little girl and the other was a monster. The nurses and the doctors wanted to take the monster away but the beautiful woman said, 'They are both my children and I will love them equally.'

The girl and the monster grew up together. Because they knew no different they assumed that every little girl had a monster to play with, and every monster had a little girl to play with. Then they had to go to school. There were no other monsters at school and they realised that it was not normal for little girls and monsters to grow up together.

The little girl enjoyed painting and dancing and singing. But the monster could not hold a paintbrush in his claws, his feet were too clumsy to dance and when he sang everyone covered their ears.

The other children were frightened. They called the monster names. Sometimes they threw stones at the monster. Sometimes the monster threw them back.

The teacher said that the monster could no longer come to school. The little girl cried but there was nothing to be done. So she left the monster behind every morning. And when she came back in the afternoon they played together under the poplars beside the river.

She had no other friends. The girls and boys at school were scared of visiting a house where a monster lived. And this made the little girl sad.

One night, however, the monster came into the girl's bedroom after dark and said, 'Come. I have something to show you.' For he could talk, despite what everyone said.

The girl placed her hand in the claws of the monster and he walked her to the open window. It was a summer night. The air was warm. And they flew. Because that's what all good monsters do with little girls in stories.

The houses were like toys below them. She could see foxes and badgers hunting in the dark. She could see water and electricity running underground. She could see the grass growing and the feel the swing of the tides. She could see the dead sailors under the sea. And when she looked up into space she felt the heat of the stars and the great spoony swirl of the galaxies and life blooming on a thousand planets.

Soon they were flying every night and she was no longer sad that she had no friends, because she had something that no one else in the world possessed.

But little girls change, and monsters change, too. The little girl was turning into a beautiful young woman. And the monster was getting bigger, with thicker fur and sharper teeth and longer claws. And changing from one thing into another is always painful.

The monster was sad. The beautiful young woman held him and he wept. He seemed so small. She stroked his fur and wiped the tears from his eyes.

'Why are you sad?' she asked.

'I don't belong here.'

'Neither do I,' said the beautiful young woman, thinking of the girls and boys at school who were not her friends.

But the monster meant something different. 'I need the company of other monsters.'

The beautiful young woman did not know that there were other monsters. She thought her monster was the only one.

'There is a place,' said the monster, 'where everyone is a monster. And in that place I am beautiful.'

'Where is this place?' asked the beautiful young woman.

'Over the hills and far away,' said the monster.

'Please don't leave me,' said the beautiful young woman.

The monster did not answer.

Sometimes, at night, when they were flying, the beautiful young woman heard growling and stamping and gnashing from over the hills and far away, but the monster said it was a dangerous place for beautiful young women and would not fly in that direction however much she pleaded.

Months passed and the nights they spent in one another's company became gradually more and more painful for them both.

One morning the beautiful young woman came to look for the monster. What she found instead was a thick, white coat lying on the floor of his room. She picked it up. It was not a coat. It was the monster's skin, a great suit of fur, with holes for the mouth and the eyes and the nose and the claws. Her monster had gone. He was beautiful now. She wept and hugged the skin then placed it gently in a drawer.

The beautiful young woman was lonely. But she was no longer living with a monster and the other children, who had also grown into young men and women by now, were no longer afraid of her.

Sometimes she missed her monster so much that she took his skin out of the drawer and pulled it on like a suit. She stood on the window and wanted to fly so badly she almost stepped off the ledge.

Then she met a handsome prince, as beautiful young women always do in stories. He loved her and she loved him, and that feeling was the nearest she had come to the way she had felt about the monster. The handsome prince said that he wanted to spend the rest of his life with her. She was scared at first, for it is hard to promise that you will do anything for the rest of your life. But he was kind and clever and he made her feel safe, so she went to live with him in his castle.

She did not tell him about the coat of fur. She lifted it from her suitcase and hid it under the bed. She tried it on sometimes when he wasn't in the house and growled and stamped and gnashed her teeth.

Often the beautiful young woman was sad. The handsome prince held her and she wept. She seemed so small. He stroked her hair and wiped the tears from her eyes.

'Why are you sad?'

'I'm a monster,' she said.

'Don't be ridiculous,' said the handsome prince.

'I used to fly,' said the beautiful young woman.

A month later the prince returned to the castle unexpectedly and found the beautiful young woman wearing the monster's skin and growling and stamping and gnashing. He was terrified. He realised that the beautiful young woman was telling the truth. She really was a monster.

He was patient and kind, however, and he tried hard to understand. But the time they spent in one another's company became gradually more and more painful for them both.

One morning he came to look for his beautiful young woman, but what he found instead was a pile of clothes lying on the floor of her room. He picked them up. Inside the clothes he found a suit of human skin, with holes for the mouth and the eyes and the nose and the fingernails. His beautiful young woman had gone.

The handsome prince was desperately lonely. He knew that he had not loved her enough. If he had loved her enough she would have stayed with him. He knew, too, that he would never love anyone ever again.

He could not bear the sight of the suit of skin. Touching it caused him pain. She would not be needing it again. So he carried it out of the castle and in the centre of the garden he built a fire and burnt the skin of the beautiful young woman until there was nothing left but ash.

Nine

Chair. A noose hanging.

Sandy Do it.

Kay No.

Sandy Do it or I'll tell Mum about you and Tina stealing money from her handbag.

Kay We didn't steal money from her handbag.

Sandy A fiver. She keeps a notebook. She thinks someone cheated her in a shop. What did you spend it on?

Kay That's none of your business.

Sandy So you did steal it. That means you have to do what I say.

Kay You're horrible and I'm not going to do it.

Sandy (*shouts*) Mum –

Kay No, stop.

Sandy Only if you do it.

Kay Why are you making me?

Sandy Because you're stupid.

Kay George is stupid and you never make him do anything like this. You just pretend to be commandos and astronauts, except no one's ever going to let you be a commando or an astronaut because you even got frightened going up that church tower.

Sandy Get onto the chair.

Pause.

Get onto the chair.

Kay *gets onto the chair.*

Sandy Now put the rope on.

Kay *puts the rope round her neck.*

Sandy   Say the words.

Kay   I don't know them.

Sandy   Say them.

Pause. **Kay** *starts to cry.*

Kay   Dear Mum . . .

Sandy   Dear Margaret.

Kay   Dear Margaret . . .

Sandy   Go on.

Kay   Please, Sandy. I can't do this. I'll do anything else. Anything else you want. Please.

Sandy   Say the words.

Kay   You're a bully. You're going to burn in hell.

Sandy   There is no hell. That's just what Mrs Atwell says to make children behave. Do it.

Kay   Dear Margaret, I hope this makes sense. My mind is not clear at the moment −

Sandy   Not wholly clear. You have to get it right.

Kay   − not wholly clear at the moment. You will know now what I have done. I apologise for the pain it will have caused you. I think you knew that this was going to happen. Maybe you are relieved that it has finally happened and you no longer have to dread it.

Sandy   I have asked God . . .

Kay   I have asked God for forgiveness. Whether I have received it I don't know. I have not heard His voice for a long time. I wish that I had been braver.

Sandy   Stronger. I wish that I had been stronger.

Kay   I wish that I had been stronger.

Sandy   Stop crying.

She can't.

Stop crying. You're not allowed to cry.

Kay   I'm going to jump.

Sandy   You're not going to jump.

Kay   I'm going to jump and I'm going to die and you'll go to prison.

Sandy   You're not going to jump. You wouldn't dare jump.

Kay   And every day of your life you'll think about me and you'll know that you killed your sister.

Sandy   Kay . . . ? Don't be stupid.

Kay   Watch me.

Sandy   Kay.

Kay   I'm going to wreck your life.

Sandy   Kay.

Margaret *enters.*

Margaret   What in God's name are you doing? Take that thing off.

Kay   He made me put the rope round my neck and he made me read out Daddy's note.

Sandy   She's lying. She just likes doing it. And she likes me to watch.

Margaret *slaps him.*

Margaret   Get out. Get out of this house. Get out now. You are evil. Do you hear me?

Sandy   He was a coward.

Margaret   Out.

Sandy *leaves.*

Margaret   If you ever do that again –

Kay   He made me do it.

Margaret   If you ever –

Kay   I'm sorry. I'm sorry. I'm sorry.

Margaret *cries.*

Margaret   I miss your father so much.

Kay *hugs her.*

Kay   It's OK, Mummy. It's going to be OK.

Margaret   You won't ever leave me, will you?

Kay   I won't ever leave you.

Margaret   Sandy's going to leave me. I know it. But I don't ever want you to leave me.

Kay   I won't leave you.

Ten

Hill. Dawn. **Kay** *sits on the ground.*

Long pause.

John *enters.*

John   Kay . . . ?

Pause.

I've been looking everywhere for you.

Kay   We think there's only one world.

John   Kay . . . ? Kay, please.

Kay   But there are so many worlds, aren't there, one laid over the other. Palimpsest. Writing over writing. Pentimento. Painting over painting. All these bluebells. Like this great wave of blue just swept in. Wind like a great, cold hand stroking the tops of the trees. There are villages underground where people lived before the birth of Jesus. Axeheads and bridles and bones. The air hums with signals. TV stations. Mobile phone calls. If we had a radio we could listen to voices talking in a hundred languages. Smell. Go on. Smell. Cut grass and loam and rotten wood. Neutrinos pouring through the earth as if the planet were made of smoke. The Great Bear. The little bear. Triangulum. Perseus. Columba. The children dreaming in their beds. Swords and sandcastles. Hammerhead sharks and drunken uncles with dirty minds.

John   You're sopping wet.

Kay   I've been out here all night.

John   Come home with me.

Kay   We have such small eyes. We think we're kings of the world. But we're like moles burrowing through all this wonder.

John   You're sick, Kay. You didn't take your medication. You haven't taken it for a week now. I found the packets. You hid them under the mattress. You need to take your medication, Kay. You need to come home with me.

Kay It's so beautiful it makes me want to cry. This is what I try to get down on paper. I thought if I came out here, if I spent the night out here, if I drank it all down . . . People don't see this. People don't feel it, they don't taste it and hear it and smell it. And I thought if I could fill myself up and take it away, then maybe I could share it, I could make people realise how many worlds there are.

John Kay . . .

Kay But there are too many, aren't there? I pick up a pen or a paintbrush, and it's all there, in my head. But as soon as I put something down on the paper I see how clumsy it is, how small, how laughable. It's just words. It's just lines. It's just colours. How can I possibly –

John Don't do this to yourself.

Kay You should come up here. Everyone should come up here. Spend a night outside. Feel the earth turning in space. Badgers. I saw badgers. I saw a deer. And bats. But people don't, do they? They're too frightened. Frightened that if they see this, if they really see it, they'll never be able to go back to their lives, because there'll be this hole inside them.

John Kay, listen. I know it's hard, but . . . just listen. The world is beautiful. And maybe I don't see that as clearly as you do. Maybe my eyes are not as open as yours. But all of this exists only because you're sitting here taking it all in. You. Kay. The person I love more than anyone in the world. And we have to look after that person, don't we? We've talked about this. There's you, and there's me, and there's this woman who is like a child sometimes. And we need to care for her. Because she's overwhelmed by all this beauty. Because she gets carried away. Because this woman sometimes has trouble looking after herself.

He touches her.

Kay (*shouts*)   Get away from me.

John   I'm not going to leave, Kay. I'm going to stay here. For as long as it takes. Because that's what we do, isn't it? That's what we do when we care for someone. That's what we do when someone's in trouble.

Kay   I'm beautiful. I really am beautiful.

Eleven

Kay and Sandy eating supper. They've been to Margaret's funeral. Kay is pregnant.

Sandy Promise me something. When I die, can you make sure that some pompous old git doesn't stand over my coffin banging on about the Kingdom of Heaven? Just stick me in the crematorium and go and get pissed, OK?

Kay I think we can arrange that.

Pause.

So, what's the gossip?

Sandy Laura and I have been seeing each other again.

Kay 'Seeing' as in 'seeing'?

Sandy We went out for a meal last month. Left the boys with her sister.

Kay A date.

Sandy She spent the night at my flat.

Kay One of those end-of-the-relationship things when you forget why you hated each other?

Sandy Maybe at first. Then we went out again.

Kay You're having an affair with your own wife.

Sandy Which turns out to be a lot more fun than being married. For her too, I think.

Kay Sandy, you have never been a leading authority on the psychology of women. Are you sure you're not stringing her along?

Sandy I asked if she wanted to get back together again and she laughed and told me not to be ridiculous. Which was a relief, to be honest.

Kay And the boys?

Sandy   I take them out most weekends. Science Museum. Millennium Wheel. Cycling in the New Forest.

Kay   My God, you're having an affair with your children, too.

Sandy   I live four streets away. It's like having a very big house. You just have to walk past the neighbours to get to the East Wing.

Kay   How is the world of industry going to survive without your hand permanently on the tiller?

Sandy   I've seen the light. I leave the office at five o'clock. Jason and Sarah do the overseas trips. And you know what . . . ? The world doesn't fall apart.

Kay   You haven't had some kind of head injury, have you?

Sandy   You're being a little rough.

Kay   Oh, I think you've got a few years of that before the scales are level.

Sandy   How are you doing?

Kay   I shouldn't really say this, but I'm good. Surprisingly good. In the circumstances.

Sandy   Well, if it makes you feel any better, I feel pretty good, too. Besides, if I'd got her to move out of that house, I'd be wondering if it was my fault.

Pause.

Kay   She spent so much of her life looking after me.

Sandy   I don't think she ever wanted you to be well.

Kay   Maybe you *are* a leading authority on the psychology of women.

Sandy   You were a project, Kay.

Kay   A bloody difficult one.

Sandy   Easier than being an artist. Easier than making something and saying, 'This is me,' and running the risk of people saying, 'No thanks.'

Kay   I wish I felt sadder.

Sandy   Bollocks. You've done enough sad for several lifetimes.

Pause.

So, what about our little passenger?

Kay   Well, I've stopped puking, for one thing. Which means I can finally leave the house without a plastic bag in my pocket.

Sandy   You're not serious?

Kay   I think I may be permanently blacklisted by Pizza Express . . . They changed my drug cocktail, which seemed to sort it out. It's a girl, incidentally. Well, they think it's a girl. Penises are easier to spot on the scan. Predictably.

John *enters with more food.*

John   Have you told him the good news?

Sandy   A girl, I hear.

John   The other good news.

Sandy   What's this?

Kay   I'm shortlisted for the Carnegie Medal.

Sandy   Is that, like, a horse race?

Kay   It's a children's book award.

John   It's *the* children's book award. Arthur Ransome. Walter de la Mare. Alan Garner. Philip Pullman. Penelope Lively.

Sandy   Well, I have heard of none of those people, but I'm assuming they are the leading lights of the book world and you're joining them. Well done, kid. I'd say you had it in you, but I didn't have a clue. How much money?

Kay   Five hundred pounds and, well, a medal, obviously.

Sandy   Bloody cheapskates. What about the spike in sales?

Pause.

OK. I'm being vulgar.

Kay (*about* **John**)   It's all thanks to this wonderful man.

John   You wrote the book.

Kay   You saved my life.

Sandy   Enough. You're going to put me off my food.

Kay   I still can't believe any of this is happening.

John   Sometimes everyone does live happily every after.

Sandy   You can do this stuff when I've gone.

Twelve

Kay *and* **John** *in bed.*

John That was . . . well, pretty fantastic, actually.

Kay And a nine-point-nine from the Romanian judge.

John You were more like eleven. Not that it's a competitive sport. That would be a very shallow way of looking at it.

Kay I'm glad I bring out the shallow side in you. You need someone to bring out your shallow side. It makes you a more rounded person.

John I suspect I was more of a six.

Kay If it was a sport I think you'd get team points rather than individual points.

John Well, I guess that makes it a . . . seven-point-nine-five average.

Kay You mean, was I any good?

John I guess I did.

Kay Did you enjoy it?

John I think you know the answer to that.

Kay Did I enjoy it?

John It certainly sounded like it.

Kay Well, that covers pretty much everyone involved.

John I just feel like an amateur. You know, in this particular sphere.

Kay Only you could use the phrase 'this particular sphere' in the bedroom.

John Sorry.

Kay No. I like it. It demonstrates your utter disregard for the passing fads of the permissive society.

John   The permissive society. Now that's not a phrase you hear much in the bedroom either.

Kay   Yes, but I was being playfully ironic. Besides . . . in my experience there is nothing worse than a man who thinks he's a great lover.

John   In your experience?

Kay   Twelve.

John   Twelve what?

Kay   Previous sexual partners. Though 'partners' is a rather grand word for three of them. Just so you don't have to feel embarrassed by having to ask the question. Which is the other question most men want to ask. After the penis-size one. In my experience. Twelve. I think that counts as woman-of-the-world without crossing the border into slut, don't you? My mother might disagree, of course.

John   I'm not sure I want to think about your mother. In this particular sphere.

Kay   And you?

John   Me what?

Kay   Previous sexual partners.

John   Well . . .

Kay   It's got to be more than one. Because you seem to know where everything is. And I don't think even you could get that from a book. And if you say ten you'll be lying because you were a bit shocked when I used the word 'cunt'. There, you see, that rabbit-in-the-headlights thing you're doing right now.

John   I don't think any of my previous partners even used the word 'vagina'.

Kay   Any of them?

John   Either of them.

Kay   I'm very glad you didn't use the word 'vagina', or I'd
think you were about to whip out a speculum.

John   What's a speculum?

Kay   Now that you really can look up in a book. So tell me
about them.

John   Tell you about who?

Kay   Now you're being deliberately obtuse.

John   Jane Halliday. Seventeen. Both of us. We were at this
party. David Carter's eighteenth. I think he's very possibly in
prison by now. We ended up doing this slow dance together.
She had these huge breasts.

Kay   Excellent.

John   They kind of blotted out all other aspects of her
character.

Kay   Come on. I want the steamy stuff.

John   I was terrified, to be honest. I think we ended up
having sex because it was the line of least resistance. You
know, when you can't think of anything to talk about and
there's this tension in the air and you're not sure if it's sexual
tension or just social discomfort.

Kay   If you're ever thinking of writing a pornographic
novel –

John   Shut up and listen.

Kay   OK.

John   We were drunk, obviously. We ended up in David's
parents' en suite bathroom. On the bath mat. Which wasn't
quite big enough, or fluffy enough. I remember feeling this
mix of pride and shame the next day. And this obligation to
carry on seeing her. Because I was rather naive and thought
we'd made some unspoken vow of commitment, and men
who dumped women after a one-night stand were cads. I had
this recurring nightmare in which she got pregnant and we

had to get married and spend the rest of our lives together. Which was not a happy thought, despite the breasts, because I was into the Logical Positivists and she liked Adam and the Ants.

Kay   I'm assuming the Logical Positivists were not a band.

John   Then her father got an engineering job in Toronto and she was completely unbothered about leaving me behind, so I felt like an idiot. And the weird thing is I suddenly did want to marry her and have children.

Kay   Number two.

John   Françoise Agnesi. Twenty-six.

Kay   Ooh. French and Italian.

John   She was a lecturer in medieval English.

Kay   My erection is wilting.

John   She was a very nice woman.

Kay   And has now almost completely disappeared.

John   Actually, she wanted me to tie her up.

Kay   This is more like it. I can see her taking off her heavy-rimmed glasses and shaking out her bun in slow motion and purring. I sincerely hope you obliged.

John   Funnily enough, she did actually have a bun.

Kay   You're not answering my question.

John   I did tie her up.

Kay   Paint me a picture. I want all the sordid details.

John   It made me feel a little queasy, to be honest.

Kay   You spoilsport. You are going to need some serious retraining.

John   You know, hurting someone. It just seemed . . . Is that something you like?

Kay   Don't you ever think about that? Being completely in someone else's power? Someone you trust. Or maybe someone you almost trust. Not having to think about anything. Not having any responsibility. Just being a body for once. Letting someone use you for their own pleasure.

John   Well . . .

He has an erection.

Kay   I don't think you're going to need much retraining after all.

John   I think you could ask me to do pretty much anything and it would have the same effect. I mean, within reason.

Kay   So what happened with you and saucy Miss Hornrims? You know, before I get the handcuffs out.

John   She was bonkers. 'Let's go to Paris. This evening. No, I've changed my mind. We can't go to Paris, I have to stay up all night marking these papers.' She bought a dog. This collie. Called it Langland. Which is not a good name to shout in a public park. Then she realised having a dog meant actually walking it twice a day and getting someone to look after it when you went away. So she gave it to these people who lived down the road. I'm not even sure they wanted a dog. She was very persuasive. She'd just light up sometimes. Then she wouldn't want to see me for days. We had these terrible arguments. She'd get so cross with me for not having strong opinions about, well, whatever she happened to have strong opinions about on that particular occasion. When it was good it was amazing. But it was bloody hard work.

Kay *says nothing.* **John** *tries to be more upbeat.*

John   On the other hand, she had pubic hair which went a freakishly long way down her inner thigh. It was like a cat sitting in her lap. There, you see, I'm loosening up already. The pubic hair of my previous sexual partners.

Pause.

What's the matter? You've gone all quiet on me. I prefer being with you in every way.

Pause.

Kay   There's something I have to tell you.

Thirteen

John *and* **Margaret**.

John   I rang Oslo. I rang Jenny. I rang her GP. I rang the hospital. I even rang that bloody hotel in Poole. No one knows anything. I have to get in touch with the police.

Margaret   Do you think you might be overreacting?

John   Kay's missing. I have absolutely no idea where she is. No one has any idea where she is. What do you expect me to do?

Margaret   Maybe she needed some time on her own.

John   She booked a plane ticket. Three hundred and thirty-seven pounds. And she never got on the plane.

Margaret   She can look after herself.

John   Margaret, there are times when she doesn't know what she's doing.

Margaret   I realise that. There are also times when you don't know what she's doing. And that's very different.

John   She's my wife. She's your daughter. She could be lying face down in a river.

Margaret   And the worst thing is that there's a part of you that longs for that.

John   There is no part of me that longs for that.

Margaret   You're lying, John.

John   Margaret . . .

Margaret   I don't tell many people this. In fact I don't think I've told anyone apart from you. But you're the only person who has some inkling of what I've been through. It's hard, isn't it? It's harder than you expected. Much harder than you can ever explain to anyone else who hasn't been through it themselves. When you love someone and they treat you like dirt. When they forget everything you did for them. When they become a different person. You want to walk away sometimes. But that would be cruel. And everyone else would know you'd been cruel, because you abandoned someone in distress. So you long for it to end. You long for it to end in a way that isn't your fault. You long for them to be found lying face down in a river, because then it'll be over, and they won't treat you like dirt any more. And everyone will feel sorry for you. It's a dreadful thing to think, a shameful thing to think, so you have to keep it to yourself, your nasty little secret. But nasty little secrets fester, don't they?

John   We all dream about stupid things, Margaret. I dream about flying. I dream about robbing a bank. I dream about shooting some of my colleagues. But that doesn't mean I'm going to do it. It doesn't even mean I want to. If she were dead –

Margaret   Do you ever hit her, John?

John   Of course I don't. Why on earth are you asking me that?

Pause.

I don't hit her.

Margaret   She's frightened of you.

John   No, Margaret. The other person is frightened of me. The person who takes her over. The person who forgets everything I've done for her. The person who thinks there are worlds upon worlds and has this supposed X-ray vision. The person who thinks she can see things the rest of us can't see. That's the person who's frightened of me.

Margaret   Her father was a very angry man . . . We say he was a good man. Because that's how we talk about the dead. Because that's how we want them to be remembered. Because I want my children to think they had a good father. And sometimes they did have a good father. But sometimes . . . he could be a monster, John.

Pause.

John   Well, maybe Sandy was the one who inherited those particular genes. And maybe Kay inherited your artistic ones.

Margaret   Really?

Pause.

I have something to show you.

John   Please . . .

Margaret *fetches* **Kay***'s artwork.*

Margaret   She wants to illustrate. She wants to write books for children.

Pause.

You might find this rather upsetting.

John   What do you mean?

But these are children's drawings. These are things she must have done when she was –

Margaret   She did these last year, John.

John   She was ill.

Margaret   She can't paint, John. She can't draw. She just thinks she can.

John   Oh my God.

Margaret   Sandy can draw. Sandy was a wonderful artist. He probably still is. Though I sincerely doubt he's put pencil to paper in the last ten years. Of course, he didn't want to be an artist. Because being an artist is soft. Because being an artist means putting yourself on the line. Because being an artist is something I wanted him to do. And Sandy has never, ever done anything I've wanted him to do.

John   I have to ring the police.

Margaret   This is what it's like, John. You think you know someone . . .

Fourteen

Train station.

Kay So, go on, tell me all about him.

John I would bore you rigid.

Kay If you can keep a bunch of students entertained . . .

John 'Entertained' is probably an exaggeration.

Kay He was a bit of a Nazi and he cried when he saw someone beating a horse and he had the most astonishing moustache.

John Two out of three.

Kay It was Wagner who had the moustache.

John No, Wagner had the sideburns. It was Nietzsche who had the moustache and cried when he saw someone beating a horse.

Kay So he wasn't a Nazi.

John He sacked his publisher because of his anti-Semitism. 'The word "German",' he wrote, 'is constantly being used nowadays, to advocate nationalism and race hatred and to be able to take pleasure in the national scabies of the heart.'

Kay 'Scabies of the heart'. Brilliant. I'm going to remember that one.

John He would have been horrified by the way his ideas were misinterpreted. Copies of *Also sprach Zarathustra* for every soldier in the First World War. *Übermensch*. He never used the word in the plural. It was about mastering one's own lesser self.

Kay You see, I find this quite sexy.

John Big moustaches and the Will to Power?

Kay Listening to you talk about stuff you really know about. Actually, listening to anyone talk about stuff they really know about. As long as they're attractive to start with. Or doing stuff they're good at. Playing the flute. Skinning a rabbit.

John Well, I guess I should be flattered.

Kay You should.

Pause.

He believed in Eternal Recurrence. Is that right?

John You see, you know more than you're giving away.

Kay He believed that everything was going to happen again and again and again, exactly the same every time.

John Correct.

Kay Except, we can't remember it happening last time, can we? So next time round we won't remember it happening this time. So it's really no different from everything happening just once.

John It's not meant literally. It's a kind of thought experiment. Can you just . . . accept all this? Can you stop longing for something better, something different? Can a demon say to you, 'This will happen over and over and it will never be different,' and you reply, 'I have never heard anything more divine'? That, he said, was the formula for human greatness.

Kay But he had a pretty crappy life, right? So it wasn't really one you'd want to live all over again.

John I think that was the point. He was physically weak. He had periods of near blindness. He suffered gastric problems and severe headaches. He thought regularly about killing himself. In 1889 he had a complete psychotic breakdown and never recovered. He must have longed desperately for something better, something different. But he couldn't have it. No one can. You can't be someone else. He dreamed of having the courage to say, 'Yes, I accept this.' He dreamed of being able to find that kind of contentment in the midst of all that suffering.

Pause.

Kay   Will you marry me?

John   I only met you half an hour ago.

Kay   I know, but will you marry me?

John   You are quite the most extraordinary woman I have ever met.

Kay   I think you need more romance in your life.

Fifteen

*Kay sleeping in a hospital bed. **John** beside her.*

John   I would have helped. You know that, don't you? I would have listened. I would have done anything. I love you so much.

Pause.

I rang your mum. She's really relieved . . . Well, obviously, she's relieved. Sorry. That's a stupid thing to say.

Pause.

The house was so empty. I kept wanting to hold you. And you weren't there.

Pause.

Jesus *enters with two coffees and a flapjack.*

Jesus   They didn't have any apple things . . . Oh.

John   I'm guessing you're not a doctor. Or maybe you are. They seem pretty informal round here.

Jesus   I'm a friend.

John   OK.

Jesus   And you are . . . ?

John   I'm Kay's husband.

Jesus   Shit.

John   Are you an old friend? Or a new friend?

Jesus   I'm an old friend. Olly. Olly Brown.

John   And you're here because . . . ?

Jesus   I brought her in. I rang for an ambulance and came with her.

John   I guess I should thank you.

Jesus Apparently she's going to be OK. She's just sedated at the moment.

John They told me.

Pause.

Jesus She didn't say anything about you.

John I've been looking for Kay for a week. I thought she was dead.

Jesus If I'd known I would have called you. I mean, I wish I'd known. Then maybe this wouldn't have happened.

Pause.

She was in a real state. I mean, before she did it.

John Well, I guessed that.

Jesus She didn't . . . I don't think she knew what she was doing. It scared the living daylights out of me. It was like she was on drugs or something. Was she on drugs?

Pause.

Sorry. I shouldn't have said that.

John I think the problem was not being on drugs.

Jesus Oh. I see . . . If I'd realised . . . She seemed so confident.

John She would.

Pause.

I don't recognise your name.

Jesus We were at college together. I was her boyfriend for a couple of terms.

John How did she find you? She hadn't seen anyone from college for years. Or was she lying to me?

Jesus She turned up at the door. Actually she turned up at my parents' door first. God knows how she remembered the address. I don't think she ever went there.

John   When was this?

Jesus   I'm really sorry.

John   When was this?

Jesus   Three days ago.

John   What did you do?

Jesus   I don't know what you mean.

John   What did the two of you do together?

Jesus   You know. Eating. Talking.

John   Three days.

Jesus   Sort of like old times. Staying up late into the night.

John   Do you have a family?

Jesus   No.

John   You slept together.

Pause.

How many times?

Jesus   It wasn't like that.

John   What *was* it like?

Pause.

Tell me.

Pause.

Jesus   We spent most of that first day in bed. Most of the second, too.

Pause.

John   We did that once. We haven't done that for a long time.

Jesus   Then something started going wrong.

John   God, I'm so tired.

Jesus   She couldn't sleep. She didn't want to sleep. She'd start reading one book, then stop and start reading another. She watched a DVD of *Magnolia*, then watched it again, straight off. I got up the second morning and she'd baked two cakes. I didn't know what to do. She seemed so happy at first.

John   Was it good sex?

Jesus   Please. If I'd known . . .

John   Tell me.

Jesus   It was good sex. It was really good sex.

Pause.

John   So what do you do?

Jesus   You mean, like, for a job?

John   Well, you can obviously take days off in the middle of the week.

Jesus   I'm an artist.

John   So you paint.

Jesus   No, no. I do video stuff. You know, these short film things . . . You?

John   I'm a philosopher. From the Greek. A lover of wisdom.

Pause.

Jesus   We shouldn't be standing here talking like this. They say people can hear, don't they? When they're unconscious.

John   I have this dream in which she does die. And the worst thing is that it's a good dream.

Jesus   Don't say that.

Pause.

John   Tell me about the two of you.

Jesus   I've said too much already.

John   I mean at college.

Pause.

Jesus   She was doing history. Obviously you know she was doing history. She was living in hall. I was living out in this shared house. Two angry feminists and this guy who did powerlifting. Kay was going out with a friend of mine.

John   Uh-huh?

Jesus   He played bass in this band. Rhinoceros. I thought I didn't have a chance. I still don't know why she went out with me, to be honest. I was shy and a bit clumsy and I still hadn't worked out who I was. I grew the hair first and spent the next ten years acquiring the bohemian lifestyle to match. But Kay . . . she was magnetic. Is magnetic. She had this light around her. You wanted it to shine on you. She was rude and funny. She made me feel like I hadn't really been alive before.

John   And then?

Jesus   That summer we went to her mother's house. This incredible lawn going down to the river. Poplars. A little weir. Forest on the far side of the valley like the Wild Wood. You know, *The Wind in the Willows*. Toad and Badger. I grew up on a council estate in Newcastle. So this was like the Serengeti. Her mother was away so we had the place to ourselves and it was fantastic. Then her mother came home. And it was good then, too. I mean, there were things we couldn't do in certain parts of the house. But we got on really well, Kay's mother and I. She was a real character. She did woodcuts, watercolours. I'd never met a real artist before. I don't think Kay was terribly interested. I mean, you just take it for granted, the stuff your parents do. She let me watch her working. It was amazing. I guess it always is. You know, watching people do stuff they're really good at. Then her brother turned up.

John   Sandy.

Jesus   He broke two of my ribs.

Pause.

She didn't come back to college. I rang her mother. She said
Kay was sick. Too sick to talk to me. I kept ringing. Her
mother cried once and asked me to stop calling. I thought
about going back to the house. But Kay telling me to go away
would have been even worse. And there was something else.
This crazy suspicion that the house wouldn't actually be there.
That Kay wouldn't be there. That none of it existed. Like a
fairy house, you visit once and then it disappears.

Pause.

I'm going.

Pause.

I don't know what to say.

Pause.

I loved her . . . When I opened that door . . . Be kind to her.

He exits.

Long pause.

Kay *comes round.*

John   Hey you.

Kay   You're here.

John   Of course I'm here.

Kay   I did something really stupid.

John   It's all right.

Kay   I thought I could fly.

John   Really. It doesn't matter.

Kay   Hospital.

John   Yep.

Kay   I've been here before.

John   Not this one.

Kay   Valium?

John   Enough to put a horse to sleep.

Kay   We had a really good time, didn't we?

John   Yeah, we've had some really good times.

Kay   I mean before this. Before I did the stupid thing.

John   We've had some wonderful times.

Kay   I mean over the last few days. We had such fun. I don't think I've had so much fun for a long, long time.

John   Kay?

Kay   What?

John   Do you know who I am?

Kay   Of course I know who you are. You're my handsome prince.

Sixteen

Darkness. **Kay** *burns her illustrations. Arctic wind. A bear in the distance, perhaps.*

Seventeen

Jesus *and* **John.**

Jesus   I have something to show you.

John   I can't do this.

Jesus   Trust me.

A decomposing body.

John   Oh shit.

Jesus   Fifteen, twenty days old. That's my guess. We're in the so-called black putrefaction stage.

Stage one is the fresh stage. It's about three days long, depending on the temperature and the surroundings. It starts with the cell walls breaking down, at which point the body starts to digest its own organs. Autolysis. This happens pretty much straight away. Under ten minutes. Acidity increases. Body temperature drops. After a couple of hours the body starts to stiffen. It's not long before you start to get flies. Hairy maggot blowfly. Beetles. Fire ants. Sometimes parasitic wasps lay their eggs in the fly pupae. The fly larvae hatch and eat the maggots alive. Sheets of skin start to come free of the flesh. Hands especially. They call it 'gloving'.

Stage two is putrefaction. The bacteria start to anaerobically metabolise the soft tissue. You get a lot of gases. The body bloats. Skin goes green. Sulphur dioxide, hydrogen sulphide, methane, ammonia. Flies, beetles, they love it. You start to get maggots in the orifices.

Stage three, black putrefaction, starts around day ten. Bloating subsides. Skin peels. Any flesh left has this soft creamy consistency. And the nails on the toes and fingers tend to come away pretty easily.

He removes one.

John   Why are you showing me this?

Jesus   This is heaven, John. There is no other place. This is not some poorly organised waiting room for a brighter, warmer, kinder world. This is all you will ever know. You can accept it or you can reject it. Which strikes me pretty much as a no-brainer. But that's just my opinion.

Stage four is butylic fermentation. That's twenty days or so. Body goes flat. Dries out. Maggots can't feed any more. So you're left with beetles and anything else which muscular jaws that can chew at the tough bits. You get a different bad smell now. Butylic acid. Same smell you get in Parmesan and vomit. You'll see hide beetles, carcass beetles, cheese flies.

Finally you go into the dry decay phase. Bones, hair, skin. No significant moisture. All the potential nutrition's been used up. At which point mummification starts. Which can carry on for . . . well, how long is a piece of string?

Pause.

This is heaven. The hurt and the rot and the cruelty and the madness. People stick hearts on Valentine's cards and get married in white dresses and give each other flowers. They think love is everything going right. That's not love. That's self-indulgence. That's good luck. Love is when you walk into the burning building. Love is when the person who means most to you in the whole world is breathing through a mask and pissing in a bag. Love is when they no longer know your name.

Pause.

I've got to go. Things to do. People to see. You look after yourself, OK?

He exits.

Pause.

A **Girl** *of eleven or twelve enters, wearing pyjamas. She cannot see the corpse.*

John   Hallo you . . . Are you OK?

Girl   I had a nightmare.

John   Do you want to tell me about it?

Girl   I was in this country, somewhere above the Arctic Circle. It was dark and cold and I was wearing a fur coat, but I couldn't feel the ends of my fingers any more. I walked and walked and I knew there was this town somewhere with golden windows. But I was terrified because I was going to freeze to death before I got there.

John   I'm so sorry.

Girl   Then I came to a tunnel in a mountain. I didn't want to go inside but I didn't really have any choice. I was hoping there were people at the end, or a fire, but it was pitch black and there was this smell like the smell of really big animals in a zoo and suddenly I could see this polar bear. A real polar bear, not like a polar bear in a storybook. It put its claw into my chest and ripped it open and my guts started pouring out. I knew that in a dream you were meant to wake up before you died. I was saying, 'You have to wake up, you have to wake up.' I was hurting really badly. And I knew you weren't meant to hurt in dreams either and I realised I was going to die and never get back to this world.

John   You're back now.

Girl   Am I? Am I really?

John   Come on. Let's take you back to bed.

Eighteen

John Traditionally we begin this morning with a rapid summary of Western philosophy. It's a bit like a coach tour of the Lake District. If you look out of the left-hand window you can see the picturesque ruins of Aristotle. If you look right you can see the rosy glow of Giordano Bruno burning at the stake. We stop at Hobbes for egg sandwiches and a Thermos of tea, then move rapidly on through Spinoza and Kant, pulling over briefly for someone to be sick into the verge at Kierkegaard.

But I'm going to assume that you already know a little bit about Western philosophy, which is why you're here, and if you don't then you can always read about it in a book, and if that doesn't appeal you can switch to geography.

Philosophy is not a body of knowledge. Philosophy is a way of being in the world. Philosophy is all about asking questions. So let's start with a big one. Why do we do philosophy?

Some people will tell you that philosophy is the fount of all knowledge. They'll tell you that psychology and sociology and linguistics all started as part of philosophy. But that's just another way of saying that philosophy is what is left over when everything useful has been taken away.

Some people will tell you that philosophy has practical applications. Artificial intelligence. Human rights. But the biggest and most difficult philosophical problems have always been the ones with no practical applications whatsoever. Do we have free will? What is knowledge?

In Plato's *Republic*, Socrates asks Glaucon to imagine a group of prisoners chained up in a cave so that they can't move or turn their heads. They're all facing in the same direction and the only thing they can see is a wall of stone. Behind them a fire is burning. In front of the fire, unbeknown to the prisoners, men pass back and forth carrying vessels and statues. The prisoners never see these men and the objects they're carrying, only their shadows on the wall. The prisoners are us. We think this is reality. But it's a puppet show, mere shadows of something brighter and more real that we can't see directly.

Philosophers have been pretty much stuck in that cave for two and a half thousand years. We've all been stuck in that cave. We have imaginations. The upside is that we've learned how to split atoms and transplant hearts and send probes to Jupiter. The downside is that we can picture ourselves being someone else, and being somewhere else. Surely, we say to ourselves, there has to be more than this. Surely there must be a larger, brighter world outside. If we could just wriggle free of our chains and turn our heads we would be able to see the vessels and the statues and the fire and the men walking back and forth and the door up into the sunlight.

There is only one undeniable philosophical truth. *Sed omnes una manet nox.* 'But one night awaits us all.' We get sick. The people we love get sick. We lose our minds. We love and we are not loved in return. There is happiness but it is fleeting and it is unpredictable and it is not under our control.

We long for something permanent, something we can rely upon completely, maybe just a few words that will remain true in spite of everything. We think of ourselves as guardians of the earth but we will blow away like thistledown. There will come a time when there is no evidence that we even existed. Is it any wonder that we yearn for some small defence against oblivion?

Does God exist? Is there a purpose to life? Can anything be known for certain? These are not academic questions. People die for these ideas. People kill for these ideas. These are the ideas we reach for in our very darkest moments and which sometimes fail us when we need them most.

Maybe you don't give a toss. Maybe you'll plod through life like cows, shitting and chewing the cud. And, Christ, there is a part of me which longs for that. No pictures in the head of other ways life might have turned out.

I wish I could just . . . I wish I could look at the shadows on the wall and stop trying to turn my head. But I can't. And those few words that will remain true in spite of everything? If only I could get them down on paper. Some small true thing. But there are worlds upon worlds and the dictionary is so small. And talking changes nothing. It all ends in the basement and I really do not think that the Goddess of Wisdom is going to intercede at the last minute.

No. Wait. Please. This is important.

I'm not making a great deal of sense. I realise that. But maybe that's good. Maybe that's more honest. Maybe that's what we should all do. Stop pretending we have the answers. Start being honest about our confusion.

Because I remember this house. I remember this house by a river. Poplars. A little weir. It's so clear and so vivid. But I have a crazy suspicion that the house never existed. I think, did this actually happen to me?

The cells of my body renew themselves constantly. My feelings change. My opinions change. I look at my memories and all I can see is a stuttering, antique film, a series of tiny photographs getting gradually more scratched and brittle. And I begin to realise that I'm just a trick of the light and the film is going to end and there is going to be nothing except the glare of the hot bulb and the bike-wheel flutter of the projector and specks of dust turning in an empty room.

'My friends walked on and I was left in fear with an open wound in my chest.' I understand the pull of north. I really do understand. Cold water and the summer sun in the middle of the night. Everything simpler and cleaner.

And I promise. I will carry on loving you when the lights go out. I will.

Nineteen

Kay *packs a suitcase.*

John *enters.*

John   What are you doing?

Kay   I'm going to Oslo.

John   Kay . . .

Kay   I haven't flown for six years. Did you know that? Of course you knew that. I used to be frightened of flying when I was a child. You know, because I thought we were going to crash. But it's stupid, isn't it? You're more likely to die falling off a stepladder. I mean, I'm obviously not going to die falling off a stepladder because I haven't been up a stepladder since 1998, but I wouldn't be scared if I did have to go up one. The safest form of travel available. Planes not stepladders. Everyone dreams of flying, don't they? It's one of those fantasies you have when you're a child. And now we can fly. And we take it for granted. Once, oh, ages ago, we were on this family holiday. Spain. Greece. Cyprus. Mum asked if we could go up to the cockpit. You could do that before 9/11. You walk up the aisle past that little doll's kitchen they have with the tiny packets of biscuits, and you go through the door and talk to the pilot and the co-pilot. Have you ever done that?

John   Kay . . .

Kay   It's so quiet up there. In the cabin all you can hear is the roar of the engines. But in the cockpit all the noise is going backwards. And the windows. They have, like, a proper window. Windscreen. Except they probably don't call it that, do they? One hundred and eighty degrees. Not that oval plexiglas thing the passengers have which is just smaller than a human torso so you know you couldn't get out of if you had to. And the clouds. These great piles, like shovelled snow. Like you're coming in to land on some alien planet in *Star Wars*.

John   Please, Kay. This is not a good idea.

Kay   Don't be ridiculous.

John   You shouldn't be going to Norway. Not at the moment.

Kay   I've got my ticket. I'm doing two interviews. I'm visiting three schools. I'm signing five hundred books.

John   I'm sure if you talk to the publisher they'll let you come another time. You don't have to tell them everything. Just say you're sick.

Kay   You're just jealous because you can't come.

John   I know you're not going to like me saying this, Kay, but you're getting really excited.

Kay   Of course I'm getting excited.

John   You're getting too excited. I know the signs. You're going to be a long way from home. There'll be no one you can talk to. Really talk to. About . . . this. If you start losing your grip, Kay, there will be no one to help and you're just going to spiral.

Kay   Stop it, John. This is a big thing for me. This is a really big thing. This is the biggest thing.

John   I know. I know. I just don't want . . . I want it to be perfect. I want it to be a good memory.

Kay   You don't like me having a life of my own, do you? You don't like me earning my own money and supporting myself.

John   This is not you, Kay.

Kay   Stop patronising me.

John   I'm not patronising you.

Kay   I need some space. Away from you.

Pause.

You fuss over me. You keep me on a leash. You want me to be your patient. You want me to be your pet. You want me to be your little girl. You don't like me having opinions. You don't like me having friends of my own. You don't like me having a part of my life that has nothing to do with you.

John   That is simply not true.

Kay   I'm not listening, John.

John   For Christ's sake, Kay. Who is going to pick up the pieces? Who always picks up the pieces? I love you, Kay. But you make it fucking hard work sometimes.

Kay   I'll phone you from the hotel.

John   Slow down. Let's talk about this. Let's think it over sensibly and logically.

Kay   Talking is all you ever do. Thinking it over sensibly and logically is all you ever do. And that might be absolutely wonderful for your students. But you know what? I find it really boring . . . I'm late.

John *grabs hold of her.*

Kay   Let me go.

John   No. Kay. Just stop for one second and listen to yourself. Does this remind you of anything? We've been here before. We've been here before way too many times. And it never ends well. And I'm not sure I have the energy to go through this again. You need to see the doctor. You need to change your meds. You need quiet. You need sleep. You need books and walks and three meals a day. Then maybe we can stop this before it gets out of control.

Kay   I am so looking forward to being in a place where I don't get this kind of shit. Now take your hand off me.

John   I can't let you go, Kay.

Kay   And how the hell are you going to stop me?

Blackout.

Methuen Drama Student Editions

Jean Anouilh *Antigone* • John Arden *Serjeant Musgrave's Dance*
Alan Ayckbourn *Confusions* • Aphra Behn *The Rover* • Edward Bond
Lear • *Saved* • Bertolt Brecht *The Caucasian Chalk Circle* • *Fear and
Misery in the Third Reich* • *The Good Person of Szechwan* • *Life of Galileo* •
Mother Courage and her Children • *The Resistible Rise of Arturo Ui* • *The
Threepenny Opera* • Anton Chekhov *The Cherry Orchard* • *The Seagull* •
Three Sisters • *Uncle Vanya* • Caryl Churchill *Serious Money* • *Top Girls*
• Shelagh Delaney *A Taste of Honey* • Euripides *Elektra* • *Medea* •
Dario Fo *Accidental Death of an Anarchist* • Michael Frayn *Copenhagen*
• John Galsworthy *Strife* • Nikolai Gogol *The Government Inspector* •
Robert Holman *Across Oka* • Henrik Ibsen *A Doll's House* • *Ghosts* •
Hedda Gabler • Charlotte Keatley *My Mother Said I Never Should* •
Bernard Kops *Dreams of Anne Frank* • Federico García Lorca *Blood
Wedding* • *Doña Rosita the Spinster* (bilingual edition) • *The House of
Bernarda Alba* • (bilingual edition) • *Yerma* (bilingual edition) • David
Mamet *Glengarry Glen Ross* • *Oleanna* • Patrick Marber *Closer* • John
Marston *Malcontent* • Martin McDonagh *The Lieutenant of Inishmore* •
Joe Orton *Loot* • Luigi Pirandello *Six Characters in Search of an Author*
• Mark Ravenhill *Shopping and F***ing* • Willy Russell *Blood Brothers*
• *Educating Rita* • Sophocles *Antigone* • *Oedipus the King* • Wole
Soyinka *Death and the King's Horseman* • Shelagh Stephenson *The
Memory of Water* • August Strindberg *Miss Julie* • J. M. Synge *The
Playboy of the Western World* • Theatre Workshop *Oh What a Lovely
War* Timberlake Wertenbaker *Our Country's Good* • Arnold Wesker
The Merchant • Oscar Wilde *The Importance of Being Earnest* •
Tennessee Williams *A Streetcar Named Desire* • *The Glass Menagerie*

Methuen Drama Modern Plays

include work by

Edward Albee
Jean Anouilh
John Arden
Margaretta D'Arcy
Peter Barnes
Sebastian Barry
Brendan Behan
Dermot Bolger
Edward Bond
Bertolt Brecht
Howard Brenton
Anthony Burgess
Simon Burke
Jim Cartwright
Caryl Churchill
Noël Coward
Lucinda Coxon
Sarah Daniels
Nick Darke
Nick Dear
Shelagh Delaney
David Edgar
David Eldridge
Dario Fo
Michael Frayn
John Godber
Paul Godfrey
David Greig
John Guare
Peter Handke
David Harrower
Jonathan Harvey
Iain Heggie
Declan Hughes
Terry Johnson
Sarah Kane
Charlotte Keatley
Barrie Keeffe
Howard Korder

Robert Lepage
Doug Lucie
Martin McDonagh
John McGrath
Terrence McNally
David Mamet
Patrick Marber
Arthur Miller
Mtwa, Ngema & Simon
Tom Murphy
Phyllis Nagy
Peter Nichols
Sean O'Brien
Joseph O'Connor
Joe Orton
Louise Page
Joe Penhall
Luigi Pirandello
Stephen Poliakoff
Franca Rame
Mark Ravenhill
Philip Ridley
Reginald Rose
Willy Russell
Jean-Paul Sartre
Sam Shepard
Wole Soyinka
Simon Stephens
Shelagh Stephenson
Peter Straughan
C. P. Taylor
Theatre de Complicite
Theatre Workshop
Sue Townsend
Judy Upton
Timberlake Wertenbaker
Roy Williams
Snoo Wilson
Victoria Wood

Methuen Drama Contemporary Dramatists

include

John Arden (two volumes)
Arden & D'Arcy
Peter Barnes (three volumes)
Sebastian Barry
Dermot Bolger
Edward Bond (eight volumes)
Howard Brenton
  (two volumes)
Richard Cameron
Jim Cartwright
Caryl Churchill (two volumes)
Sarah Daniels (two volumes)
Nick Darke
David Edgar (three volumes)
David Eldridge
Ben Elton
Dario Fo (two volumes)
Michael Frayn (three volumes)
David Greig
John Godber (four volumes)
Paul Godfrey
John Guare
Lee Hall (two volumes)
Peter Handke
Jonathan Harvey
  (two volumes)
Declan Hughes
Terry Johnson (three volumes)
Sarah Kane
Barrie Keeffe
Bernard-Marie Koltès
  (two volumes)
Franz Xaver Kroetz
David Lan
Bryony Lavery
Deborah Levy
Doug Lucie

David Mamet (four volumes)
Martin McDonagh
Duncan McLean
Anthony Minghella
  (two volumes)
Tom Murphy (six volumes)
Phyllis Nagy
Anthony Neilsen (two volumes)
Philip Osment
Gary Owen
Louise Page
Stewart Parker (two volumes)
Joe Penhall (two volumes)
Stephen Poliakoff
  (three volumes)
David Rabe (two volumes)
Mark Ravenhill (two volumes)
Christina Reid
Philip Ridley
Willy Russell
Eric-Emmanuel Schmitt
Ntozake Shange
Sam Shepard (two volumes)
Wole Soyinka (two volumes)
Simon Stephens (two volumes)
Shelagh Stephenson
David Storey (three volumes)
Sue Townsend
Judy Upton
Michel Vinaver
  (two volumes)
Arnold Wesker (two volumes)
Michael Wilcox
Roy Williams (three volumes)
Snoo Wilson (two volumes)
David Wood (two volumes)
Victoria Wood

Methuen Drama World Classics

include

Jean Anouilh (two volumes)
Brendan Behan
Aphra Behn
Bertolt Brecht (eight volumes)
Büchner
Bulgakov
Calderón
Čapek
Anton Chekhov
Noël Coward (eight volumes)
Feydeau
Eduardo De Filippo
Max Frisch
John Galsworthy
Gogol
Gorky (two volumes)
Harley Granville Barker
    (two volumes)
Victor Hugo
Henrik Ibsen (six volumes)
Jarry

Lorca (three volumes)
Marivaux
Mustapha Matura
David Mercer (two volumes)
Arthur Miller (five volumes)
Molière
Musset
Peter Nichols (two volumes)
Joe Orton
A. W. Pinero
Luigi Pirandello
Terence Rattigan
    (two volumes)
W. Somerset Maugham
    (two volumes)
August Strindberg
    (three volumes)
J. M. Synge
Ramón del Valle-Inclan
Frank Wedekind
Oscar Wilde

Methuen Drama Classical Greek Dramatists
include

Aeschylus Plays: One
(Persians, Seven Against Thebes, Suppliants,
Prometheus Bound)

Aeschylus Plays: Two
(Oresteia: Agamemnon, Libation-Bearers, Eumenides)

Aristophanes Plays: One
(Acharnians, Knights, Peace, Lysistrata)

Aristophanes Plays: Two
(Wasps, Clouds, Birds, Festival Time, Frogs)

Aristophanes & Menander: New Comedy
(Women in Power, Wealth, The Malcontent,
The Woman from Samos)

Euripides Plays: One
(Medea, The Phoenician Women, Bacchae)

Euripides Plays: Two
(Hecuba, The Women of Troy,
Iphigeneia at Aulis, Cyclops)

Euripides Plays: Three
(Alkestis, Helen, Ion)

Euripides Plays: Four
(Elektra, Orestes, Iphigeneia in Tauris)

Euripides Plays: Five
(Andromache, Herakles' Children, Herakles)

Euripides Plays: Six
(Hippolytos, Suppliants, Rhesos)

Sophocles Plays: One
(Oedipus the King, Oedipus at Colonus, Antigone)

Sophocles Plays: Two
(Ajax, Women of Trachis, Electra, Philoctetes)